Essex County Council

ENDANGERED ANIMALS in the RIVERS

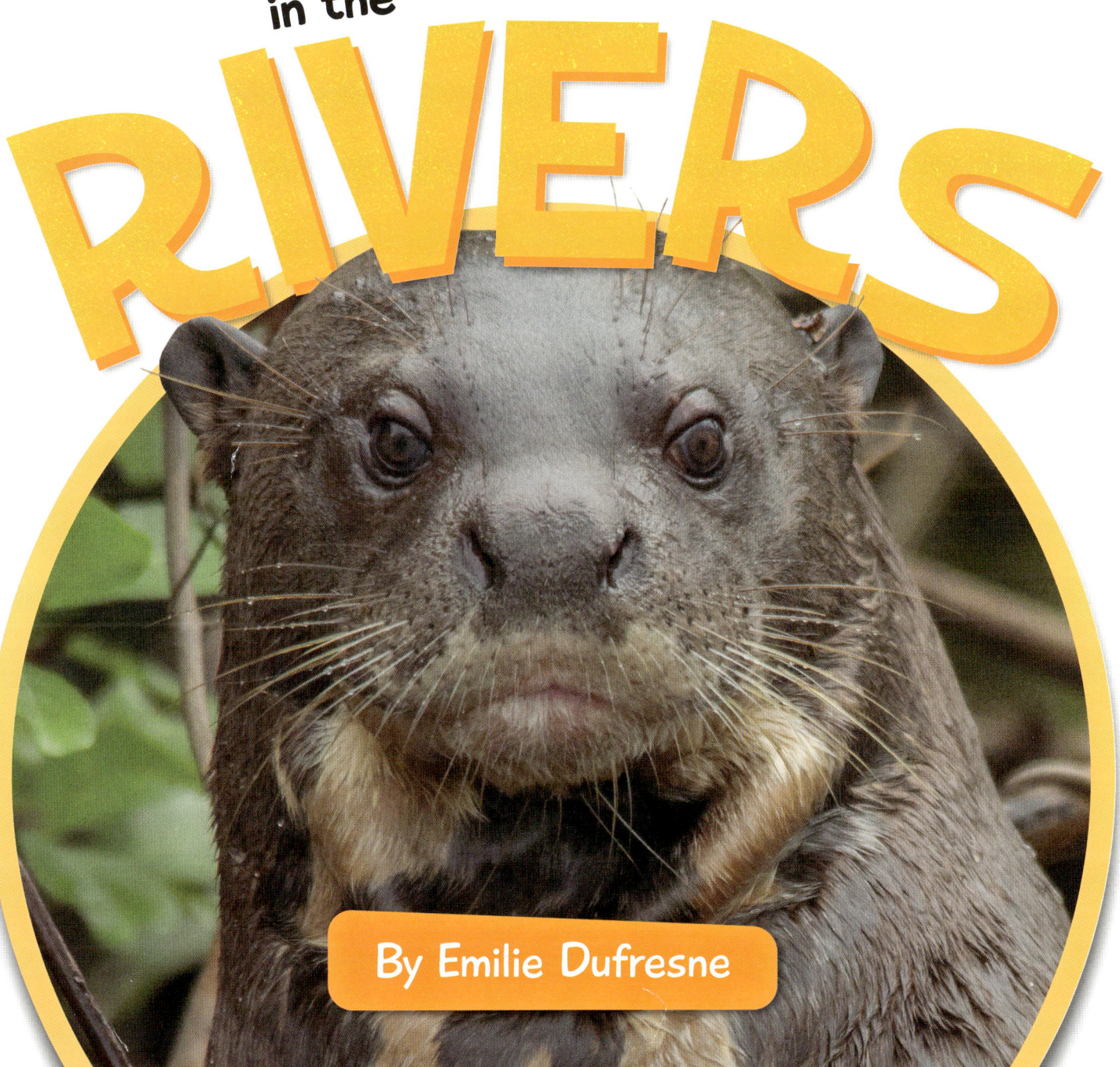

By Emilie Dufresne

BookLife PUBLISHING

©2021
BookLife Publishing Ltd.
King's Lynn
Norfolk PE30 4LS

All rights reserved.
Printed in Malta.

A catalogue record for this book is available from the British Library.

ISBN: 978-1-83927-464-0

Written by:
Emilie Dufresne

Edited by:
Madeline Tyler

Designed by:
Jasmine Pointer

All facts, statistics, web addresses and URLs in this book were verified as valid and accurate at time of writing. No responsibility for any changes to external websites or references can be accepted by either the author or publisher.

PHOTO CREDITS

All images are courtesy of Shutterstock.com, unless otherwise specified. With thanks to Getty Images, Thinkstock Photo and iStockphoto. Cover – COULANGES, s.tomas, Moehring. 4–5 – Vaclav Sebek, juerginho. 6–7 – PablitoStock. 8–9 – Merkushev Vasiliy, GoncharukMaks, Gary Saxe. 10–11 – Tatiana Belova, PhotoStock10, Artem Nechaev. 12–13 – COULANGES, A7880S. 14–15 – Mike Towers, Bill Roque, REVector. 16–17 – Martin Pelanek, Samuel Bloch, Gallinago_media. 18–19 – OSTILL is Franck Camhi, jo Crebbin, Alewtincka. 20–21 – Unknown author / CC BY-SA (https://creativecommons.org/licenses/by-sa/4.0), Alneth / CC BY-SA (https://creativecommons.org/licenses/by-sa/4.0), Shane Gross, Osama Attia. 22–23 – Surkov Vladimir, Gonzalo Buzonni, Volodymyr Plysiuk.

CONTENTS

Page 4   Being Endangered
Page 6   A Closer Look at the Categories
Page 8   The River Habitat
Page 10 Stellate Sturgeon
Page 12 Amazon River Dolphins
Page 14 Mekong Giant Catfish
Page 16 Black Stilts
Page 18 Giant Otters
Page 20 Now Extinct
Page 21 Success Stories
Page 22 Save the Animals!
Page 24 Glossary and Index

Words that look like <u>this</u> can be found in the glossary on page 24.

Being ENDANGERED

When a <u>species</u> of animal is endangered, it means that it is in danger of going extinct. When a species is extinct, it means there are no more of that animal left alive in the world.

Polar bears are an endangered species.

There are lots of different reasons that a species might become endangered. For example, if a species' <u>habitat</u> becomes <u>polluted</u>, it could become endangered.

Great white egret

Rubbish

Humans are polluting the habitats of many river animals with things such as rubbish and <u>chemicals</u>.

A Closer Look at the CATEGORIES

Different species are put into different categories depending on how <u>threatened</u> they are.

Data Deficient – Not enough information to know what category the species is in

Least Concern – Currently not in danger of going extinct

Near Threatened – Likely to be threatened soon

Vulnerable – Facing a high <u>risk</u> of extinction in the wild

Always check this website to find the most up-to-date information...

www.iucnredlist.org

Endangered — Facing a very high risk of extinction in the wild

Critically Endangered — Facing extremely high risk of extinction in the wild

Extinct in the Wild — When a species can no longer be found in the wild and only lives in <u>captivity</u>

Extinct — When a species no longer exists in the world

The RIVER HABITAT

Rivers are large bodies of running water. Rivers are freshwater habitats. This means the water is not salty.

Mountain

River

Rivers often start on high land, such as a mountain, and end when they reach a lake or ocean.

Ocean

There are lots of different river habitats all over the world. The animals that live in these rivers are specially <u>adapted</u> to live there and <u>rely on</u> them to survive.

River dam

Many river animals face challenges such as the building of <u>dams</u> and loss of habitat.

STELLATE STURGEON

Stellate sturgeon are being overfished and poached. This means too many fish are caught and there is not enough time to replace them through <u>breeding</u>.

NAME:
Stellate sturgeon

FOUND:
Mainly the Caspian Sea and Ural River

CATEGORY:
Critically endangered

Poaching is when an animal is hunted and killed, even though it is against the law.

- Stellate sturgeon found

Dams such as this one on the Danube River block the journey of stellate sturgeon.

Humans have also built dams on the rivers where stellate sturgeon usually breed. This blocks the stellate sturgeon from travelling to their normal breeding rivers.

11

Amazon River
DOLPHINS

Humans use dangerous chemicals that end up in the Amazon River. The chemicals make their way into the Amazon animals through their food.

- Amazon river dolphins found

The chemicals build up in river animals and can be very dangerous to them.

Amazon river dolphins can also get caught and die in fishing nets.

NAME: Amazon river dolphin

FOUND: Rivers across the Amazon

CATEGORY: Endangered

Amazon river dolphins are also poached by people. Their rotting meat is then used to help people catch other fish.

Mekong GIANT CATFISH

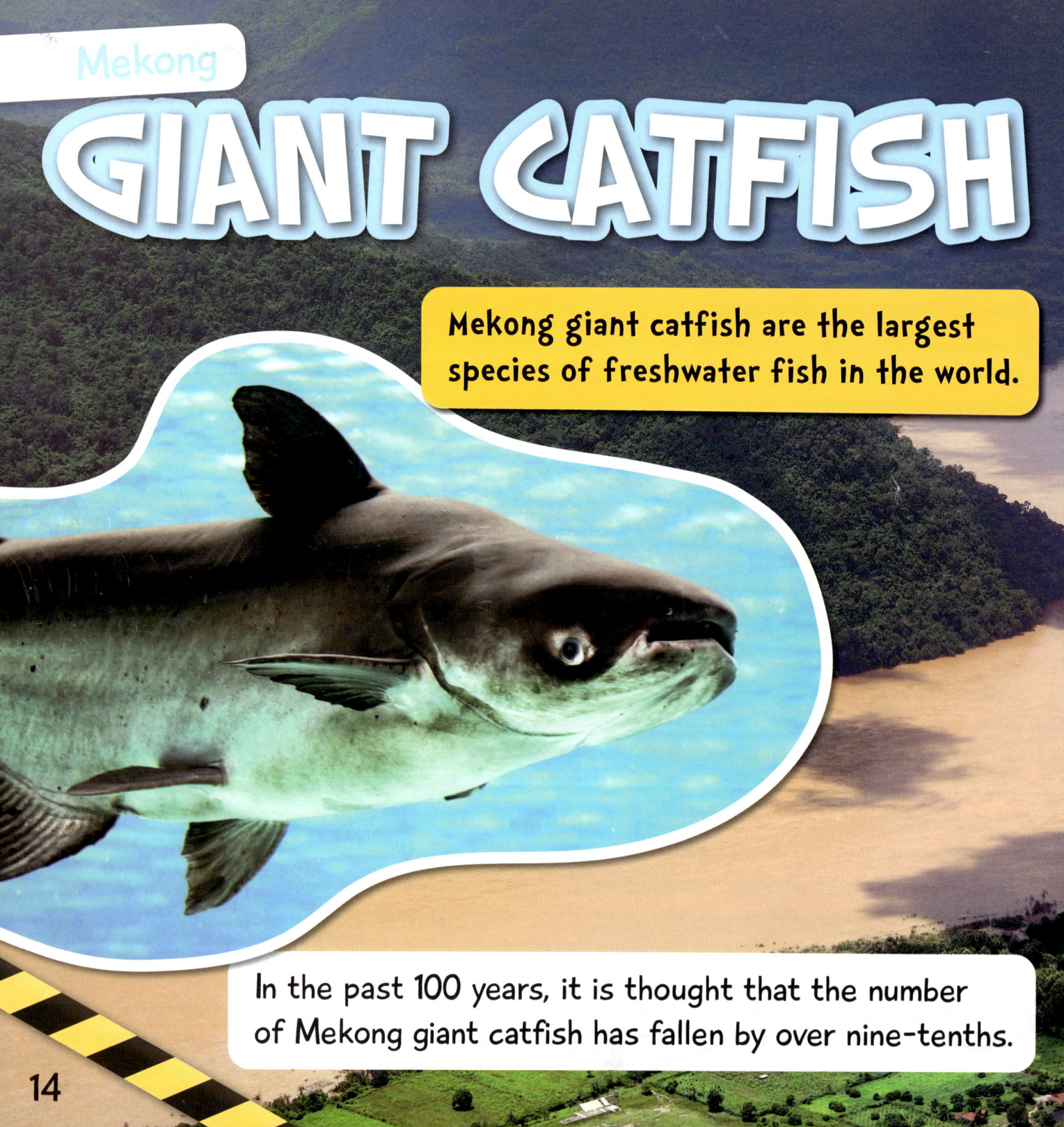

Mekong giant catfish are the largest species of freshwater fish in the world.

In the past 100 years, it is thought that the number of Mekong giant catfish has fallen by over nine-tenths.

Like many other freshwater fish, the Mekong giant catfish is in danger of losing its habitat. This is because lots of dams are being built along the Mekong River.

Mekong River

NAME:
Mekong giant catfish

FOUND:
The Mekong River (Laos, Thailand, Cambodia, Vietnam)

CATEGORY:
Critically endangered

- Mekong Giant catfish found

When dams are built along the river, it doesn't leave much space for catfish to live and breed.

BLACK STILTS

NAME:
Black stilt

FOUND:
Rivers, streams, ponds and swamps in New Zealand

CATEGORY:
Critically endangered

Black stilts are threatened by introduced animals. These are animals which did not originally live in the same habitat as the stilt but were brought in by humans.

Introduced animals such as cats, ferrets and stoats all hunt and eat black stilts.

Black stilts are also critically endangered because a lot of their habitat has been turned into farming land.

Black stilt found

It is thought that there are fewer than 100 black stilts left in the wild.

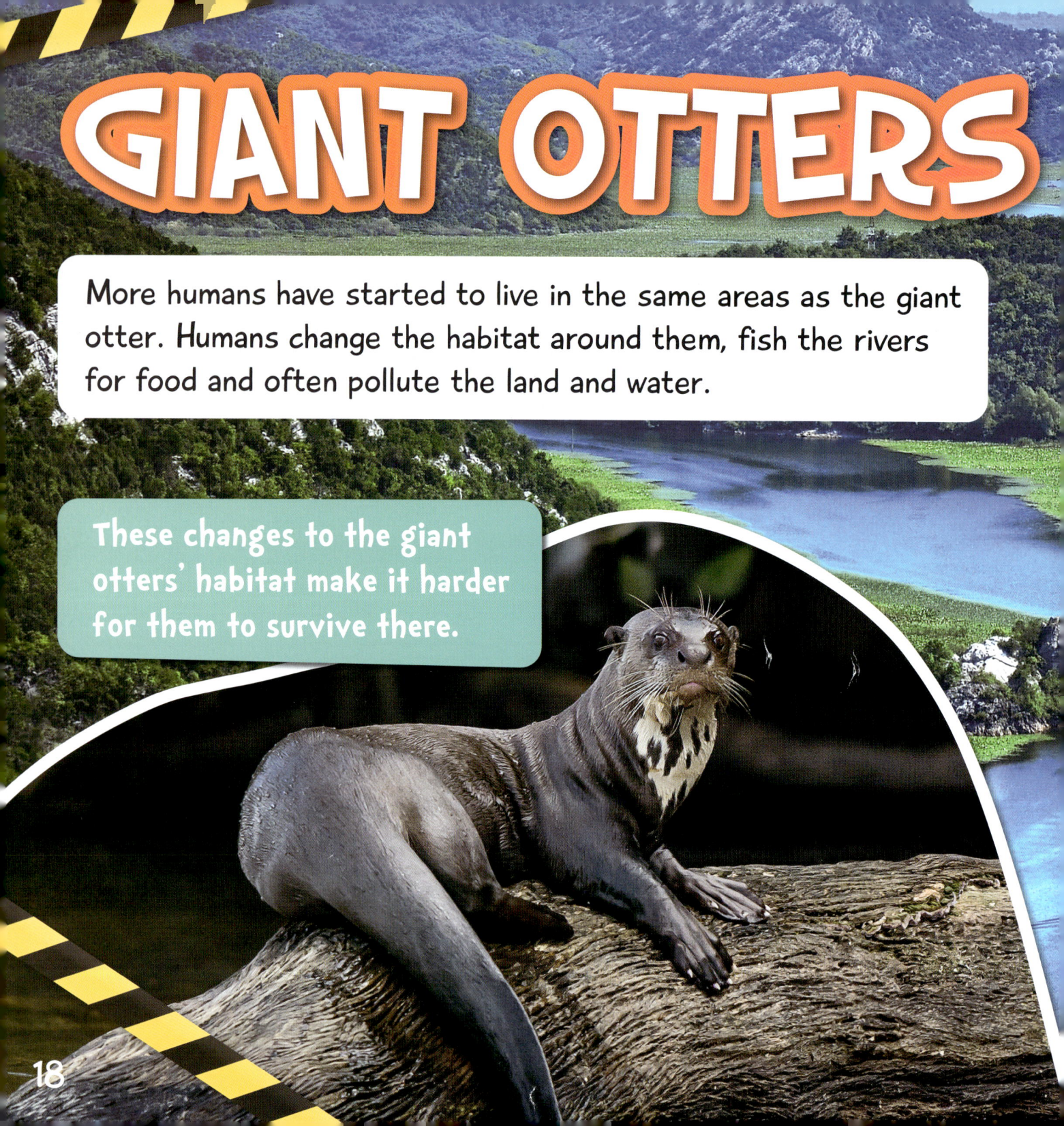

GIANT OTTERS

More humans have started to live in the same areas as the giant otter. Humans change the habitat around them, fish the rivers for food and often pollute the land and water.

These changes to the giant otters' habitat make it harder for them to survive there.

NAME:
Giant otter

FOUND:
Rivers across the Amazon

CATEGORY:
Endangered

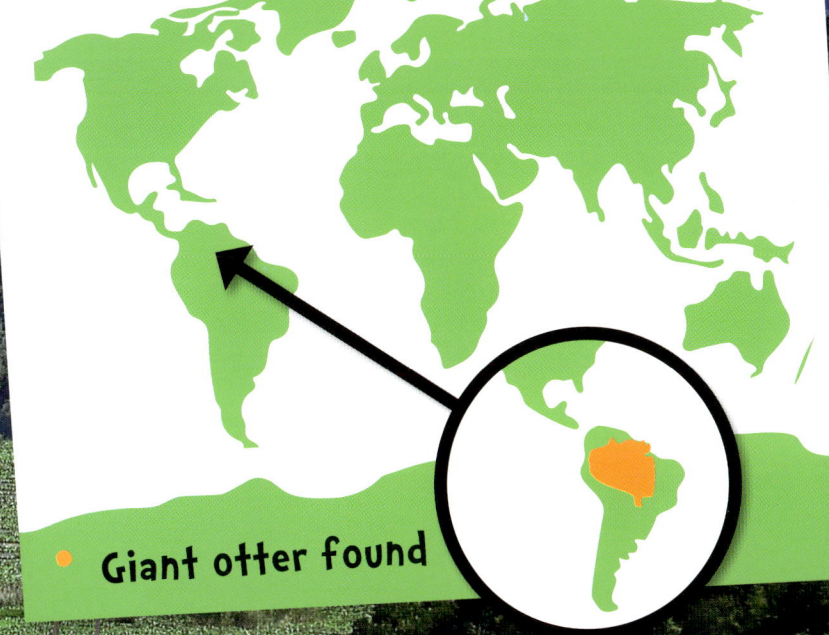

Giant otter found

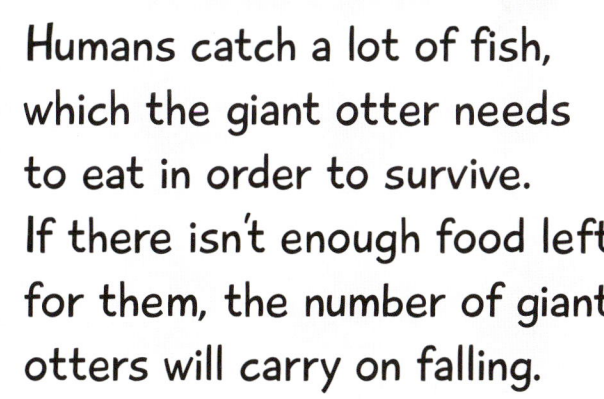

Humans catch a lot of fish, which the giant otter needs to eat in order to survive. If there isn't enough food left for them, the number of giant otters will carry on falling.

In the past, many giant otters were hunted for their fur.

NOW EXTINCT

BAIJI

The last sighting of a baiji was in the 2000s and they are now thought to be extinct.

CHINESE PADDLEFISH

The last Chinese paddlefish was seen in 2003. Nobody has seen one since then and they are now thought to be extinct.

SUCCESS STORIES

The American crocodile was losing lots of its habitat because of human action. Now, lots is being done to look after the habitat and actually create more habitats for them.

Their numbers are now increasing.

SAVE the ANIMALS!

There are lots of things you can do to help endangered river species around the world.

RIVER CLEAN-UP

Rubbish pollution is a big problem for river animals. You could visit a local river with your friends and family to do a river clean-up.

Don't forget bin bags and gloves!

JOIN FRESHWATER FORCE

Ask your parents to sign up for the WWF's Freshwater Force. This group fights for the protection of freshwater habitats across the world.

Go on this website and search for Freshwater Force for more information!

support.worldwildlife.org

GLOSSARY

adapted	when an animal or plant has changed over time to suit where it lives
breeding	when two animals create young together
captivity	kept in a zoo or safari park and not in the wild
chemicals	things that are usually made by scientists
dams	barriers that hold back the water in a river or stream
habitat	the natural home in which animals, plants and other living things live
polluted	made harmful or dirty through the actions of humans
rely on	need in order to survive
risk	when there is a chance that something might happen
species	a group of very similar animals or plants that can create young together
threatened	not sure of whether a type of animal or plant will survive

INDEX

Amazon, the 12–13, 19
critically endangered 7, 10, 15–17
dams 9, 11, 15
endangered 4–5, 7, 13, 19, 22
farming 17
fishing 10, 13, 18–19
fur 19
habitats 5, 8–9, 15–18, 21, 23
humans 5, 11–12, 16, 18–19, 21
hunting 10, 16, 19